This book offers a wealth of simple and inexpensive ideas to amuse your toddler and to encourage him/her to become a *Supertot* – a happy, confident child, eager to discover the world. Games for indoors and out, water play, singing and dancing, toys to make, books to read, are among the many suggestions to aid and abet the often harassed toddler parent or caregiver.

# SUPERTOT

Other books

by Jean Marzollo
   illustrated by Irene Trivas

Superkids (Unwin Paperbacks)


by Jean Marzollo and Janice Lloyd
   illustrated by Irene Trivas

Learning Through Play (Unwin Paperbacks)

# SUPERTOT

## A Parent's Guide to Toddlers

## By JEAN MARZOLLO

## Illustrated by IRENE TRIVAS

**London
UNWIN PAPER BACKS**
**Boston**          **Sydney**

First published in Great Britain by George Allen & Unwin, 1980
First published in Unwin Paperbacks 1984
Reprinted 1984 (twice)

**UNWIN ® PAPERBACKS**
**40 Museum Street, London WC1A 1LU, UK**

Unwin Paperbacks
Park Lane, Hemel Hempstead, Herts HP2 4TE, UK

George Allen & Unwin Australia Pty Ltd,
8 Napier Street, North Sydney, NSW 2060 Australia

©1977, 1980 and 1984 by Jean Marzollo and Irene Trivas
First published in the USA by Harper & Row Publishers Inc.

British publication rights arranged with Sheldon Fogelman.

**British Library Cataloguing in Publication Data**

Marzollo, Jean
  Supertot.
1. Education, Preschool    2. Domestic education
3. Play
I. Title    II. Trivas, Irene
649'.5 HQ774.5
ISBN 0-04-649026-4

Typeset in 11 on 13 point Century Schoolbook
Printed in Great Britain by
Guernsey Press Co. Ltd, Guernsey, Channel Islands

# Dedicated to
# all the supertots we know

Special Thanks:

To the Marzollos—
my husband, Claudio,
my children, Danny
and David, and my
in-laws, Veglia and
Dick—for their love
and help in writing
this book.

To my mother, Ruth S. Martin,
for being a mother who
likes to read poems aloud
and make things by
hand.

To Dr. Dorothy H. Cohen
of Bank Street College
of Education for her
supportive discussions
about parenting and
early childhood education.

Jean Marzollo

To my New York family:
Rose, Rachel, David
and Michael Weil,
and to my friends
in Vermont
with love and
gratitude.

Irene Trivas

# Contents

# Introduction

What makes one- to three-year-olds both wonderful and frustrating is that they want to learn about everything: people, clothes, food, furniture, tools, cars, animals, books, grass, sticks, flowers, dirt—you name it—if they can get their hands on it, if they can just *see* it, they are interested. To them, the world is brand new, and they are experiencing it for the first time. By the time they are three years old, they will have spent more than a thousand days examining what's around them; they will have absorbed a good deal of information and come to some conclusions of their own about the fruits of learning, conclusions that may stay with them for the rest of their lives.

Unfortunately, some children will conclude that curiosity leads to trouble and that questions annoy adults. They will have discovered that the safest and most pleasant way to get through a day is to maintain the status quo. Some children will have turned into monarchs, more preoccupied with ruling their families than with anything else. Others are more fortunate. By the age of three these lucky ones will have concluded that learning is a busy and joyful business that brings personal rewards as well as appreciation and encouragement from the people they love.

These children are supertots; by the age of three they will have developed a

positive attitude towards themselves, life, and learning that will enrich their entire lives. All this by the age of three; yet, oddly enough, most books on play and early learning do not specifically describe appropriate learning activities for one- to three-year-old children. Infanthood is stressed, as are the years from three to eight, but the general feeling parents often pick up from reading books written by child psychologists and educators is that the best thing for one- to three-year-olds is to stay close by their mothers at home so that they can soak up security for the school years to come.

Something's wrong with this kind of thinking. Personally, I think it has been promoted largely by male paediatricians and academicians who are not at home with their children on a full-time basis. Talk to most mothers of one- to three-year-olds about their waking hours and they will tell you that they and their children get bored being home all day long together. They get bored with their home, their things, and each other. That they love each other is not in dispute: that they are content merely to relish the warmth and security of each other all day long is.

I believe that it is necessary and important to provide stimulating play situations for one- to three-year-old children. Doing this takes skill, forethought, and organization, but in the long run, the effort is worth it for both you and your child. It is not easy to be the parent of a supertot. One- to three-year-olds are known for their terrible, negative moments. The phrase "terrible twos" comes from the experience many parents have with children who seem to defy any and all efforts toward peaceful, pleasant negotiations. The energies that supertots devote to learning can drive you crazy at times; for you too have personal needs—the need to be quiet sometimes, the need to keep certain rooms tidy sometimes, the need to get out and be with other adults.

Supertots don't care much for your needs. When they get older, they may understand, but now they just want someone to play with. In the struggle between meeting your child's needs and your own, don't give up on yourself. Get organized to do both. Teach your child to enjoy playing alone sometimes. Get good babysitters who will keep your child safe and happy when you're not there. Get together with friends to form a mother and toddler club. Why, I often wonder, do so many books on child psychology suggest waiting until a child is three before arranging for him or her to play in a nursery school setting with other children? My own experience has been that co-operative groups run by parents are greatly enjoyed by many one- to three-year-olds. (See Chapter 10 for suggestions on how to start one.) It's true that small children don't play together the way older ones do, but they love to investigate each other's toys, and they like watching one another in action.

The purpose of this book is to suggest specific learning activities that supertots like. The main intention of each idea is to help children develop some aspect of their potential. The goal is personal, never competitive. A supertot is not necessarily the smartest, toughest, fastest child in the street, but one who feels loved, likes the world, and continues to want to learn about it.

Another intention of the activities is to give parents a break. When you want to do something with your child, or when you are busy and need to find something for your child to do, consult the book quickly. Use it as a recipe book of practical ideas. The illustrations are provided to show you how the activities work and to convey the idea that perfection is not expected.

In order to help you make the most of the ideas, however, the following advice is given to help you develop the art of teaching your own child. For after all, the home really is the child's first school, and you really are your child's first teacher. In saying this, I hasten to point out that by "school" I don't mean contrived, formal lessons, and by "parents as teachers" I don't mean strict, stereotyped schoolteachers. The kind of education that is needed in the home is a gentle and joyous and casual kind of education that goes on as naturally as conversation and play. For that is precisely it: conversation and play are the two main ingredients of high-quality education for supertots.

To teach your child in the best way, you must first learn to identify and support your child's investigations. Watch. What is your child interested in at the moment? The cat? The fringe on the couch? The new toy that Grandma brought? Whatever it is, allow your child to find out more about it, provided the investigations are safe.

Second, talk about whatever it is that interests your child. Name it, describe it, ask questions. Talk *with* your child, not *at* him or her. Don't overdo it. Try to guess what your child would like you to say or tell about. If you think he or she would like you to be quiet, be quiet.

Third, introduce new experiences at the right moment. If your child is absorbed in watching the cat, don't distract him or her by calling attention to the new toy. Wait until an appropriate moment comes.

Last, enjoy your child and don't be pushy. The developmental stages of growth for so-called normal children unfold in a general plan that enables you to make some comparisons with other children of the same age. For example, between ten and fifteen months most children learn to walk. But the specific timetable is individual, and you'll only waste time and energy competing with others and trying to get your

child to do something before he or she is ready. You're not that powerful, and thank goodness you aren't. It would be awful to be totally responsible for every bit of progress your child makes. Too many parents today feel needless anxiety about the developmental progress of their children.

Which leads back again to your happiness and sense of well-being as a person and parent. What you feel about yourself is an important part of what you convey each day to your child about people and life. The more you feel a sense of your own worth, the less apt you will be to use your child to compete for you and make you happy. As you take loving care of your child's emotional, physical, and educational growth, take loving care of yourself too. Give yourself rights as a person: even the right to resent being a parent sometimes.

Some parents think learning is something that happens in the brain only. They think "educational toys" promote learning better than anything else. They are misinformed. Learning for children involves the whole body: eyes, ears, mouths, teeth, hands, feet, tummies, arms, and legs. All parts of the body need to be valued and exercised.

Learning involves emotions too. Learning how you feel about something is especially important to very young children who have already experienced a full range of emotions before they are able to identify them. Learning that others, especially you, share the same kinds of comfortable and uncomfortable feelings is crucial. Learning to trust others is essential for developing attitudes about the outside world and wanting to learn more about it. In short, all aspects of your child's growth are important: intellectual, creative, social, emotional, and physical. As parents of a supertot, you can foster a balanced development for your child; I hope this book will help you.

**1.**

252

super-stition (s·ū·
super-tot´(-tŏt´)·

super-vi·sion
su·per-vi·so·ry

# Chapter 1
# Definition of a Supertot

You may already have a supertot and not know it. If your one- to three-year-old is normally curious and active, you probably do, but I hate that word "normal"; it connotes the perfect child, an impossible and therefore misleading image. Your child was born with a potential for learning that if fulfilled will be a source of enormous personal satisfaction. A supertot feels good about him- or herself and is able to develop his or her potential. Sounds simple, but it's not; for one reason or another, many young children do not have the opportunity in their first, formative years to be supertots.

# How to know a supertot when you see one

A supertot is
one to three years old.

A supertot likes
him- or herself.

A supertot is
curious.

A supertot is
creative.

A supertot is
active.

A supertot
loves to learn.

17

# Watching supertots grow

In the time from twelve to thirty-six months supertots change dramatically in the way they can use their fingers, arms, legs, mind, emotions, and powers of communication. They change along amazingly predictable lines, sharing a loose, natural, inner timetable with other children their own age. Parents often feel better when they see the timetable written down in front of them; it helps them to recognize and welcome their child's accomplishments when they occur. It also helps them to be alert to new developments. But if parents find that their child doesn't fit any one description snugly, they shouldn't worry (unless there are clear indications of developmental difficulties, in which case, parents should bring these problems to the attention of a doctor). The important thing to keep in mind is that each child moves along at his or her own speed. It does no good to push or pull, so relax; enjoy your child's developments as they unfold, and before you know it your child will have grown up.

16–17 months

### 12–13 months

At this age, most children like to creep, crawl, or walk about, sit on the floor and pivot around while playing with toys, hold and let go of small objects, put things in their mouths, use their fingers, say two or three words, put two different syllables together (ba-da), and be hugged.

### 14–15 months

At this age, most children like to stand up and sit down, practise walking, drop toys from their high chairs to get attention, look for hidden toys, play Peek-a-Boo and Arms Up/Arms Down with you, try to pull off their socks, feed themselves with their fingers, say four to five words, and understand other words.

At this age, most children like to crawl upstairs and down, throw objects, squat down and pick things up, walk around carrying things, play with sand and water, roughhouse with you, fill up and empty containers, stack two or three blocks, try feeding themselves with a spoon, drink from a (two-handled) training cup, respond to your words, point to show you what they want, wave bye-bye, say five to seven words, and understand more.

## 18–20 months

GIMME DAT!

At this age, most children like to run (though awkwardly), pull and push things around, throw things, walk upstairs, "dance" to music, fetch things and carry them to you, make a tower of three or four blocks and knock it over, try to turn the pages of a book, take things apart, insist on feeding themselves, point to and name parts of the body, hum and sing, use a vocabulary of ten to twelve words, use words to tell you what they want (Gimme dat, Need dat, Mine), say their favourite word (No), cuddle a teddy bear, and get their own way.

WHAZZAT?

## 21–23 months

At this age, most children like to walk upstairs, kick a ball, climb up on to and down from chairs, sort objects and shapes, colour with crayons, fit things together, peel a banana, point to things and ask "Whazzat?", say short sentences, and use a vocabulary of about twenty words.

CAR GO BOOM!

## 24–26 months

At this age, most children like to run around, walk backwards, make non-pedalling riding toys go fast, do very simple puzzles, put pegs in peg board, hammer pegs, play with dolls, take off their shoes, imitate the way adults talk and act, follow simple commands (Please bring me the doll), talk about themselves in the third person (Dougie go out), use more words and longer sentences.

DAVID FIXIN' RADORATOR!

**27–29 months**

At this age, most children like to jump, turn door knobs, imitate the play of older children, draw with crayons, unscrew nuts from bolts, unbutton large buttons, eat well with a fork, listen to sounds and guess what made them, and understand up to three hundred words.

I PUT DOLLY UP THERE

**30–35 months**

At this age, most children like to walk up and down stairs easily, climb things and jump off, walk on a smooth plank raised a few inches off the ground, match objects of a similar colour, try to hold a crayon properly, wash and dry their hands, avoid known hazards (the street, matches), try to dress themselves, sing the words of several songs, learn rhyming jingles, understand a vocabulary of up to 450 words, count to 10 or 20 as a chant (without knowing what the numbers mean or how they are used), talk with you, and carry out established routines.

I BLOW CANDLES LIKE THIS... YOU SEE, MUMMY?

**36 months**

At this age, most children like to ride a tricycle, climb a jungle gym, string beads, build a bridge from blocks, take turns with other children as long as their turn comes often enough, feed themselves neatly, understand explanations, tell their names and addresses, play baby sometimes, imitate grown-ups, and carry on extended conversations with you.

21

# Chapter 2

# Supertots and Language

Of all the things that supertots learn, language is the most remarkable. Think of it: at the age of one a child can say only two or three words, but at three the same child has a vocabulary of up to a thousand words—words to ask questions, give explanations, describe things, express feelings, greet people, fantasize, and sing. The world opens up with words.

But knowing the meanings of words does not necessarily give children the ability to communicate. They have to learn to pronounce them, make sentences with them, and to *listen* to the words of others. They have to want to use words, want to talk, and feel that others want to talk with them. Over and over again, all day long, day after day, you have the opportunity to talk casually with your child and convey the sense that communication between people is a vital part of life.

# How to teach your child to talk

Talk about things *before* your child learns to talk.

Be interested in your child's first sounds.

Don't talk baby talk.

DA BA

DA BA

Ba-ba

Ba-by

MA-MA

DA-DA

Bye-bye

KA!!

When your child starts making two-syllable sounds with each syllable sounding different, enjoy this amazing progress and talk back.

A magic moment occurs when your child, with your help, connects sounds he or she makes with people and objects in the outside world. Soon your child has a working vocabulary, and you can really talk together. True, you may only have five shared words at this point, but the list will grow rapidly if you enjoy talking together.

# Talk about the world around you

Talk with your child and listen to his or her comments, be they babbling sounds or real words. Sometimes, when your child gets better at saying real words, you can correct the pronunciation; but, in general, forget about perfection and let your "conversations" come naturally. New words, phrases, and eventually sentences will be learned by your child at his or her own speed in his or her own time. The main thing is attitude: your child should feel that he or she wants to talk with you and that you want to talk with him or her.

# Talk about what you see your child doing

Good teachers know the secret of learning; there's no good reason why you shouldn't know it too. After all, it's true that parents are a child's first teachers.

Learning takes place when a child *wants* to learn something and the teacher *knows* what the child wants to learn and *helps*.

Sounds simple, but it's not; helping children learn is an art. You cannot make your child learn something unless he or she wants to. So wait, listen, watch, and think about what's going on when your child is playing. Then, when you get on the same wavelength, make a few suggestions.

YOU WANT TO KNOW SOMETHING YOU CAN DO WITH THOSE STICKS?

YOU CAN POKE THEM IN THE SAND LIKE THIS. SEE? THEY LOOK LIKE TREES!

# Talk about routines

Children like their daily routines, and they like to talk about what's familiar. Conversation with them can make certain boring routines more interesting to you.

### Waking up
How many ways can you say hello?

### Getting dressed
This is a good time to talk about colours, stripes, buttons, zips, previous owners of hand-me-downs, and pictures on jerseys.

### Papers and post
Deliveries present an opportunity to talk about the postman, the post-van, the paper-boy, and what came today: letters, parcels, magazines, newspapers, leaflets, and stamps.

### Washing hands
Think of all the words you can teach: clean/dirty, before/after, finished/not finished, all done/not all done, wet/dry.

## Mealtime

Tastes, smells, colours, textures, cooking tools, eating utensils, feeling hungry and feeling full: there's a lot to talk about at mealtime.

## Nap time

Talk about what you did this morning and what you'll do together *after* the nap.

## Going out

Kids like to repeat the names of everything being put on them and why.

## Tidying up

Think of picking up as a long-range goal that is taught in small incremental steps. Don't ask for too much too soon, but get the point across that toys eventually have to be picked up and that you will help.

# Chanting

Supertots love to repeat things over and over again. This talent can drive you crazy unless you find a way to live with it. Making up chants is one way. You start, and your child listens and joins in. Here are a few basic chant patterns to use in different situations.

## Variations

The Who-wears-mittens Chant:
> Daddy wears mittens.
> Mummy wears mittens.
> Matt wears mittens.
> Becky wears mittens.
> And who else?
> Teddy wears mittens.

The Who-gets-mad-sometimes Chant:
> Daddy gets mad sometimes.
> Mummy gets mad sometimes.
> Grandma gets mad sometimes.
> David gets mad sometimes.
> Eva gets mad sometimes.
> Even Mr Rogers gets mad sometimes.

# How to chant a child out of a "no-mood"

**THE BIG NO**

DO YOU WANT TO PLAY BALL?
NO

NO BALL... HMMM. DO YOU WANT TO COLOUR?
NO

NO COLOUR... HMMM. DO YOU WANT TO RIP UP MAGAZINES?
NO

NO RIP... HMMM. DO YOU WANT TO MAKE A TOWER?
NO

NO TOWER... HMMM. DO YOU WANT TO READ A BOOK?
NO

NO BOOK... HMMM. DO YOU WANT TO PUT ON A SWEATER?
NO

NO SWEATER... HMMM. DO YOU WANT TO PUT ON YOUR BRAND-NEW BRIGHT-RED COWBOY HAT?

YES!

**HINT**

**Hint:** Don't start "dressing chants" unless you're prepared to say them *always*. For example: *Red shirt today? No. Green shirt today? No. Blue shirt today? No.* This can be a drag.

**VARIATION:** IS IT A

Is it a dog?
No.
Is it a pig?
No.
Is it a cow?
Yes.

31

# Fingerplay games

Remember "Incy Wincy Spider"? That's an example of what teachers call "fingerplay games". Children love them, and they don't seem to mind if they can't manipulate their fingers and hands as well as you can.

**Two Little Dickie Birds** (spoken, not sung)

Two little
dickie birds
Sitting on a wall;
One named Peter,
One named Paul.
Fly away, Peter;
Fly away, Paul;
Come back, Peter;
Come back, Paul.

## Where is Thumbkin?

(sung to the tune of "Frère Jacques")

Where is Thumbkin?
Where is Thumbkin?
Here I am.
Here I am.
How are you today, sir?
Very fine and thank you.
Run away,
Run away.

VERSES

Use a different finger for
each verse, as follows:

1. Thumbkin = thumb
2. Pointer = first finger
3. Tall man = second finger
4. Ring man = third finger
5. Pinky = little finger

WHERE IS THUMBKIN?
WHERE IS THUMBKIN?

HERE I AM.

HERE I AM.

HOW ARE YOU TODAY, SIR?

VERY FINE AND THANK YOU.

RUN AWAY.

RUN AWAY.

TUM...

# Love letters out loud

You can never say "I love you" too many times. Young children soak up love, storing reserves of it for insecure moments. Every day you can say these things; one day perhaps you'll hear some of them said back to you.

# Playing baby

As supertots get older, they sometimes like to play baby. The nice thing about playing this "game" with your child is that you acknowledge his or her periodic returns to babyhood and teach your child that inner feelings are something that you can handle.

# Expressing different kinds of emotions

Your child will start feeling emotions long before he or she can explain or discuss them. You can help by talking naturally about your own feelings so that he or she will learn that different emotions are something that everybody experiences.

# Why?

WHY DO I HAVE TO HAVE A NAP?

WHY?

One day it will happen. Your child will start asking you *why. Why do I have to have a nap? Why do I have to eat fish fingers? Why are you going out? Why is Grandma sleeping?* You feel honour-bound to offer reasonable explanations so that your child will catch on to the order of things. *You need to nap so you won't be tired later this afternoon. You need to eat fish fingers because they're good for you. I'm going out to the shop to buy some milk. Grandma is sleeping because she's very tired.* That's enough. Longer explanations are tiresome; children want to know a lot but not very much in depth. If they keep on asking why, keep answering in simple sentences. But if you sense that they're asking just to get your attention, then say so and get out of the trap by giving your child some undivided attention or by saying *"Because"* and changing the subject.

# 3.

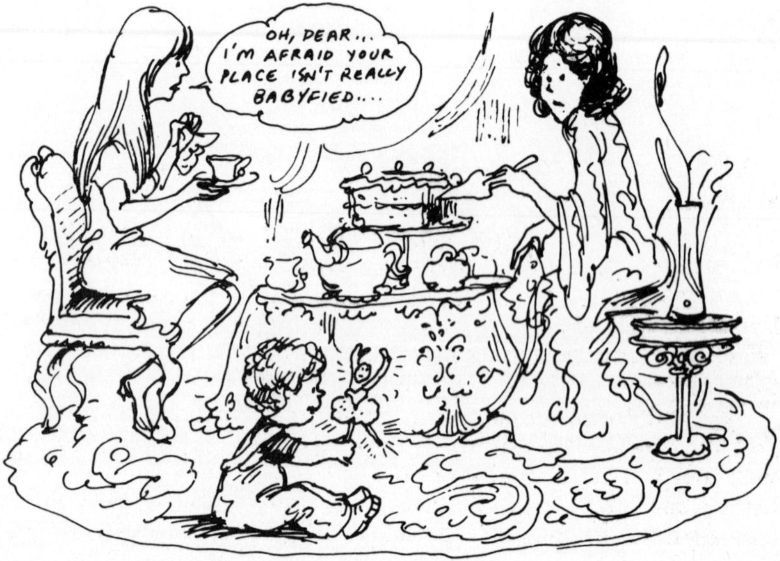

# Chapter 3
# Favourite Things to Do

Basically, supertots want to explore their own environment, preferably with you or someone else to share in the fun. If they can't persuade you to play *with* them, they want you nearby to help when they need you. Usually they won't play by themselves in another room, which is fine, because not until they are almost three can they be trusted to play alone safely, and even then not for very long.

Some of the things supertots do not want to do are: play with toys they can't work, play in places where there are too many things they can't touch, be made to play with something a certain way by an over-zealous adult, and be interrupted in the middle of an activity in which they are involved. Some of the things they do like to do are shown on the following pages.

# Water play

PLANT SPRAYER

In addition to being highly educational, playing with water in the kitchen sink, bath, or outdoor paddling pool is, for most children, bliss. Until your child learns a few precautionary rules, stay close by and participate. Rules depend on your child's abilities and where he or she is playing; some rules might be: *don't touch the hot water tap, don't throw water on the floor, don't stand up in the bath, don't splash people*. Once your child knows the rules, stay nearby to make sure everything is safe and okay, but let him or her play essentially alone, with a few occasional suggestions from you.

## Favourite water play activities

NOW KEEP STILL, DOLLY.

Giving the doll a bath and shampoo.

Pouring from and filling up containers— "washing dishes".

KEEP IT IN THE SINK, DAVID... ...SO I SAID TO HIM...

Give your child plastic bottles and dishes to wash, and let him or her use whatever you use to wash them, a sponge or dishcloth. If your child is using the sink, be sure he or she is standing on a safe chair with arms. Stay nearby to keep an eye on things.

# Water play toys

SPONGES

2 LITTLE PLASTIC BOTTLES THAT FIT HAND EASILY (OLD PILL BOTTLES ARE GOOD)

BATH TOYS

TEA STRAINER

PLASTIC MEASURING CUP + SPOONS

ONE CUP
ONE HALF
QUARTER

SQUEEZE BOTTLE

PLASTIC EYE DROPPER

PLASTIC FUNNEL

PLASTIC CONTAINER WITH HOLES PUNCHED IN SIDE

CLEAR FLEXIBLE TUBING

# Sand play

Sand play, like water play, is a first-rate activity for supertots. It is creative, educational, and fun. Two rules should be taught: *don't eat sand and don't throw it*. To teach the rules, stop the undesired behaviour when it starts, say the rule firmly, and suggest or show an alternative sand activity.

An easy way to make a sandbox is to fill an old tyre or plastic paddling pool with silver sand taken from a clean beach or bought from a garden centre or educational supplier, or from a builder (but be sure to ask for *washed* sand). Turn a larger plastic pool over the sandbox at night to keep rain and animals out. The larger pool can be used for paddling and water play during the day.

# What supertots like to do in a sandbox

*With dry sand*

 Use scoops and shovels to fill containers.

 Pour sand out of containers.

 Load up well-designed, easily dumpable dumptrucks and then dump them out.

 Make designs with sandcombs cut from cardboard (parent has to cut them).

 Sweep up (if sandbox is inside or on patio).

*With wet sand*

 Mix water and sand.

 Mould things (an adult probably has to help); a good mould for a supertot is a paper cup because it is lightweight and small enough to hold in one hand.

 Pat, shape, tunnel, poke.

 Stick twigs and pebbles into wet sand (don't suggest pebbles if your child is likely to eat them).

 Draw lines with sticks (teach your child to be careful with sticks, and don't leave a child unattended while playing with them).

# Play near you

Supertots like to have things to do in the kitchen so they can be there when you're there. A low, easy-to-open cupboard filled with stuff is fun, especially if you change the contents around so that your child never knows what to expect. Some things you can put in there are: magazines, ragbooks, clean plastic bottles and containers, paper bags, toys, and an assortment of wrapping paper and scrap paper for tearing up.

# Try to help you

Children love to imitate you. If you provide them with small, safe replicas of the tools you use, they'll be delighted to work alongside you.

# Cooking

Cooking . . . sort of. The point is: children watch *you* cook and would like to try it too. Here are some safe, simple, and relatively mess-free "recipes" for them.

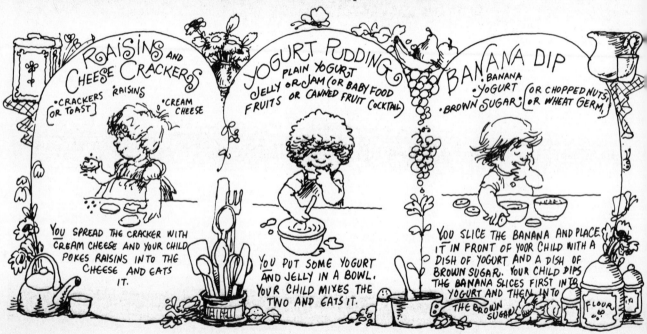

**RAISINS AND CHEESE CRACKERS**

- CRACKERS (OR TOAST)
- RAISINS
- CREAM CHEESE

YOU SPREAD THE CRACKER WITH CREAM CHEESE AND YOUR CHILD POKES RAISINS INTO THE CHEESE AND EATS IT.

**YOGURT PUDDING**

PLAIN YOGURT
JELLY OR JAM (OR BABY FOOD FRUITS OR CANNED FRUIT (COCKTAIL)

YOU PUT SOME YOGURT AND JELLY IN A BOWL. YOUR CHILD MIXES THE TWO AND EATS IT.

**BANANA DIP**

- BANANA
- YOGURT
- BROWN SUGAR (OR CHOPPED NUTS OR WHEAT GERM)

YOU SLICE THE BANANA AND PLACE IT IN FRONT OF YOUR CHILD WITH A DISH OF YOGURT AND A DISH OF BROWN SUGAR. YOUR CHILD DIPS THE BANANA SLICES FIRST INTO YOGURT AND THEN INTO THE BROWN SUGAR.

# Homemade foods

Instant foods teach children that juice comes from cans, cakes from paper bags, and peas from cardboard boxes. Every now and then, make something from scratch with your child.

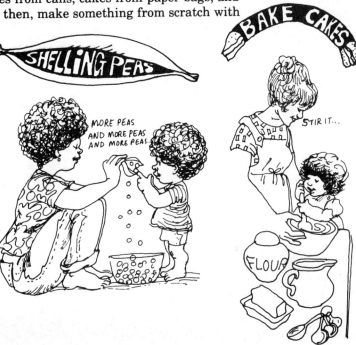

If you have a garden, grow some lettuce and tomatoes. True, most supertots aren't crazy about salad, but at least they'll know where it comes from.

# Outdoor play

Ideally, a supertot's play area would contain:

- · a safe place to run around.
- · a safe place to climb up and slide down
- · a safe place to use riding toys
- · a safe place to play with sand
- · a safe place to swing
- · a safe place to play with water
- · a comfortable place for adults to sit and watch

One- and two-year-olds cannot be trusted outside alone. They wander off to explore new ground, and they lack a sense of what might be dangerous even in their own garden or park. You or a babysitter must watch them. To give yourself a break, make a large fenced-in area in the garden. If the phone rings, you can run inside for a moment and watch your child from the window. If friends drop round, you can sit with them outside and still keep an eye on your child. If you do build a fence, think of the area inside of it as a playground. Provide various spots of interest and activity. Be sure everything is safe. You can buy various types of fencing at garden centres or do-it-yourself stores. Don't buy anything too expensive if its purpose is just to fence in the play area; by the time your child is three, he or she won't stay in it.

49

# Crawl around on the ground with you

Although your child has probably passed through the crawling stage by the time you start to use this book, crawling practice is still good exercise. Some neurologists feel that cross-pattern crawling (opposite hand moves at the same time as the opposite knee) is necessary for full brain development. The mental ability to direct such a complicated set of actions as are required for crawling is strengthened by lots of crawling practice and may later be used for other kinds of complicated skills such as reading and writing. Crawling around on all fours may not look like a pre-reading activity, but some educators think it is.

# Be quiet together

One- and two-year-olds like to alternate active, noisy, and busy periods of play with quiet, restful moments. When you go out, whether it be to the park or garden, bring along a few things for quiet times.

# What about TV?

Most supertots like to watch TV, and for short periods each day watching TV can be a valid diversion. After a period of active exploration and free play, for example, a child may enjoy watching a suitable TV programme. On their part, the parents are relieved that their child is safe, quiet, and learning something; but parents do have to be careful. Too much TV trains children to be TV zombies.

**How to turn your child into a TV zombie**

Let him or her watch
TV all day long.

Let him or her watch it
in a restricted place
(high chair or playpen) so
there is no alternative
but to watch.

Don't discuss anything
with your child. Don't
watch TV with your child.

Let your child watch anything.

By the time your TV zombie starts school, he or she will have spent more hours watching TV than university graduates spend getting their degrees. TV zombies often have trouble at school because they are fidgety, clumsy, and easily distracted. Add up the hours. Two hours a day, seven days a week, is fourteen hours of TV a week. That's enough; indeed, many educators would say that's too much for young children, who learn not from TV but from moving around and playing with real things.

You may notice that young children often watch TV for only short periods. After they have wandered off and become engaged in another activity, turn the TV off. Don't have the noise a constant part of the auditory background in your home. *That* will teach your child how not to listen to what's going on. On the other hand, some children like certain portions of a show but dislike others. Be sure they have toys around so they won't learn to watch what bores them.

If you let your children watch TV (many educators think you shouldn't), be sure to teach them how to watch it. Attitudes about discriminating viewing can be learned early. Children can learn about the medium itself as well as the content of any show, but you will have to help. Talk about TV and TV shows with them.

SOMETIMES TV IS BORING. LET'S TURN IT OFF AND PLAY CARS.

YEAH.

# Chapter 4
# Making Toys Together

Once upon a time, children had very few shop-bought toys; they made do with sticks and stones, and they had larger families to amuse them. Today, with so many good toys available, parents have come to rely on them to entertain and teach their children. Three things are lost in this development: a certain spirit of resourcefulness that comes from needing something and having to make it, the intimate joy that comes from making something with someone else, and finally the satisfying sense of process you get when you see an idea become a real thing.

Parents do well to set aside time with their children to improvise toys from the environment around them. Sometimes this takes a special effort, for almost always there's a commercial toy that will do the job better. You can't buy the process of making a toy, however; you can only experience it together.

Because, at this age, supertots can't make things very well by themselves or sit for very long watching you make something, the projects have to be simple. As you start them, keep in mind the goal: you want your child to acquire a taste for homemade things to counterbalance that other taste he or she is rapidly developing: the taste for buying things.

# Toys from nature

THIS IS THE MUMMY LEAF...

With so many toy shops around, it's easy to overlook natural toys outside.

| | | |
|---|---|---|
| Pine cones | Sticks | Crab shells |
| Acorns | Pebbles | Sea shells |
| Seeds | Logs | Feathers |
| Nuts | Leaves | Grass |

You and your child can collect natural toys in the woods, in the park, on the beach, and in the garden. When you go for walks, take along a plastic container or small paper bag to hold whatever you find.

When you get home, sort out your treasures, and when you have finished playing with them, store them in containers for future play. Don't let seeds and pebbles get sprinkled around the house, where they turn from treasure to rubbish.

NOTE:
If your child still puts things in his mouth, postpone these collecting activities a while, or supervise closely. Meanwhile, teach that sea shells, pebbles and seeds are for touching and playing, NOT FOR EATING. Some leaves, berries and seeds are poisonous.

# Three things to do with natural toys

## Make a sea shell sculpture

You need:
- white glue (washable, usually labelled PVA)
- sea shells
- small pieces of unsplintery wood (optional)
- cardboard

Pour a little glue into a small plastic saucer. Show your child how to dip the sea shells and wood into the glue and stick them on to the cardboard. Your child will get glue on his or her clothes and hands. It will wash off. Extra glue dripped on the cardboard will harden and dry.

## Build a pine cone pyramid

Build it, then knock it over. (An adult or older child will be needed to get the pine cones into a pyramid of architectural perfection.)

## Make a rattle

Put pebbles or sea shells into an empty metal tin with safely rounded edges and a snap-shut lid. Let your child experiment with different sounds by putting in different things to rattle around.

# More things to do with stones and nuts

Fill up a baking
tray (the sort used
for small cakes)
with pebbles.

Pour nuts into
a box and take
them out again.

Poke stones into
a small hole cut
in a cardboard box.

Make a "train" out of stones.

Fill a pie-dish
with acorns.

# Cardboard tube slide

Supertots love to see things go in one end of a cardboard tube and come out the other end. The longer the tube, the better.

HERE COMES ANOTHER ONE!

# Cardboard tube rattle

Seal the bottom of a cardboard tube with masking tape. Let your child "help". Pour in about ¼ cup of dried lentils, rice, paper clips, or anything else you can think of that will rattle around and make a noise. Seal the top. When interest in the rattle wanes, help your child take off the tape and return the contents to their original source or rubbish bin. Teach your child not to eat the rattle or the contents.

# Nesting tins

Save different-sized tin cans to make a nesting game. Cut the tops or bottoms off cleanly so there are no jagged edges, or put adhesive tape around the edges to make them smooth. Nesting tins can be stacked and knocked over with a loud satisfying crash. Store the tins, when they're not being used, in a low kitchen cupboard accessible to your child.

# What to do with boxes

THIS ONE FITS, TOO...

Cut a hole in a box and find toys small enough to go inside.

Colour a box. It feels different from paper.

A big box can be a
house, shop, car,
train, or boat.

# Batman capes

Children don't have to watch Batman to know about him; they learn all they need to know from older children. Batman is special and has power; therefore, it's fun to run around wearing a Batman cape, yelling "Batman!" You can make your child a simple Batman cape out of blue cloth. Iron-on Batman insignias can be bought at some stores or toy shops.

PS: This is a great birthday present to make for a child aged from two to five. It's probably too old for children younger than two.

SEW

RIBBON TO TIE AROUND THE NECK.

18"

12"

# Doll ponchos

Small children who experience being dressed and undressed by big people every day love to dress and undress little dolls. The trouble is, though, that at the age of one and two, children don't have the manual skills to manipulate the commercial doll clothing that comes with most shop-bought dolls. As a result, doll dressing becomes an activity that children can't really enjoy until they are older. You can make simple doll ponchos that your child will be able to put on his or her dolls very easily. You might also want to make a big poncho for your child.

**How to make a doll poncho:**
Cut a hole and slit in the centre of a rectangle of fabric. No sewing is required.

**Make different ponchos for different purposes:**

White—doctor/nurse
Blue—policeman/policewoman
Wool—for cold weather
Cotton—for warm weather
Long—gown
Short—shirt

CUT HERE ON SOLID LINE

FOLD

# Paper picture jigsaws

Take a fairly simple magazine or calendar picture that your child likes and cut it into four parts. Then, help your child put it back together again.

This is a quiet, intimate activity that you can do with your child during the hour before bedtime, just after his or her nap, or on a rainy day. If you stick clear perspex on the front of the picture or thinnish cardboard on the back before you cut it into pieces, you can save the puzzle for another time.

## Caution:

Teach your child not to use your scissors: if he or she wants to cut, provide a pair of small, blunt scissors especially made for children.

# Inside-outside game

To make this, cut flaps on a large sheet of paper, as shown. Tape the paper with the flaps to another sheet of paper. Write a number on top of each flap. Lift up the flap and draw as many dots underneath as are indicated by the number on the flap.

While playing this game, don't expect too much: developmentally, you child is not yet ready to *understand* numbers. But he or she may be able to recognize numerals for their shape and may like to pretend to count the dots underneath. Small children today hear a lot about counting from TV and from older children; they like to pretend they know what it's about. You can pretend with them.

**5.**

# Chapter 5
# Selecting Toys to Buy

You don't need to buy a lot of toys for your child, but you probably will, regardless of your income level. On birthdays and holidays most children are given large numbers of toys with warm and loving enthusiasm from parents and relatives who enjoy giving them. Since you and they are going to spend the money anyway, why not buy toys that your child will like and that won't break when they're played with?

The recommendations in this chapter, which can help you with your selections, may often seem advanced for the stages that supertots go through; but children get more out of toys they grow into than toys that arrive too late to be challenging. If you do buy a toy that seems too advanced for your child, don't force him or her to use it in any particular way. If it's a slide, for example, don't demand sliding; when your child is ready, he or she will learn to slide. For now, the slide can be a slope to roll balls down and a place to crawl under.

# Toys for a one-year-old

### Stacking rings

Your child won't be able to stack the rings in the correct order until he or she is two and a half or three; but now he or she will like to hold them, throw them, teethe on them, and watch older kids and parents stack them correctly.

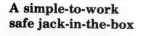

### A simple-to-work safe jack-in-the-box

The box should open easily enough for your child to do it alone.

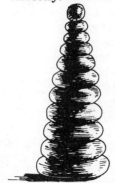

### Snap-lock beads

These colourful, plastic beads are pretty and fun to hold. One-year-olds can't snap them yet, but they like to pull them apart and throw them about.

### Bath toys

Most supertots like an assortment of floating toys for the bath. (Be sure to supervise your child when he or she is playing in water.)

### Small boats for the bath and paddling pool

Small fat ones with no small dangerous parts to be pulled off are good. Fisher-Price makes an inexpensive set of three bath boats with people that fit inside them.

## Climbing frames/slides

Versatile climbing frames and slides are very expensive, but many parents think they are worth the money because they interest children for several years. In the long run they provide more pleasure than a lot of small, cheap toys that can get lost or broken. Children can learn to slide when they're fourteen to eighteen months old.

## Toy telephone

Supertots like to imitate their parents on the phone.

## Toy house and people

Sturdily constructed dolls' houses that open up come in various shapes and sizes. Choose tough, chunky furniture and a variety of play people, animals and cars. Alternatively, to save money, you can buy the people and furniture, but make a house yourself out of wood (well sand-papered and painted or varnished to avoid splinters) or improvise one out of a strong cardboard box.

## Small riding toys

Supertots can paddle along before they can pedal. They begin to enjoy riding toys when they are fourteen to eighteen months old.

# Toys for a one-and-a-half-year-old

## Shape toys

Children enjoy putting three-dimensional shapes into something (a special post-box, toy shoe, or box) into which matching holes have been cut. They take the shapes out and put them in again—a perfectly satisfying activity as long as the shapes aren't too difficult.

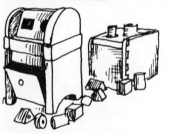

## Teddy bear

A one-and-a-half-year-old can begin to develop an emotional attachment to a teddy bear. Be sure the bear is safe and well made; it may get a lot of wear. The eyes and nose should be embroidered on securely; there should be no buttons to chew off and swallow. Don't buy a wind-up, musical teddy bear; it's not as cuddly, and any small mechanism could come out and get swallowed.

## Big wooden beads

Fat, easy-to-hold beads are fun to hold and drop into containers. An older child or adult has to help with the stringing.

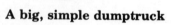

## A big, simple dumptruck

A one-and-a-half-year-old should be able to fill the truck and dump it easily. Don't buy a dumptruck that has a lot of little plastic parts that break off easily.

72

## Play-Doh

Play-Doh, a non-toxic modelling clay, can be re-used if you store it in airtight jars. Kids like Play-Doh because it's soft. Parents like it because it's less messy than real clay. Some people prefer dough made with three cups of flour, one cup of salt, and enough water to mix it into a soft pliable lump.

## Barn and farm animals

Children like animals and enjoy putting small, realistic ones into a barn or box.

## Alphabet or number blocks

Young children like these cubic, hand-sized blocks for stacking and dropping into containers. You may like the letters, but don't expect your supertot to do much more than recognize a few of them. Spelling comes later.

## Push-and-pull toys

Supertots like to push and pull this kind of toy around, especially if it makes a noise. Sometimes they pretend the toy is a vacuum cleaner or lawnmower.

# Toys for a two-year-old

### Safe riding toy

One of the most fun is the Mothercare polythene tractor. Kids push it with their feet, steer easily, and rarely fall off.

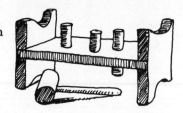

### Art Supplies

See Chapter 6 and page 163.

### Cobbler's bench

Supertots pound the pegs through to the other side, then turn the bench over and pound them back.

### Play House

The Fisher-Price Play Family House is one of the best toys in the Play Family line. The house opens out for free play with the five-member family, every room is fully furnished and decorated, there is a car in the garage, and the front door, garage door and cupboard door under the stairs open and shut. A special carrying handle locks the house with all the pieces safely inside.

### Doll

Both girls and boys need dolls to love; and fortunately, for little boys, Bambola now make a doll (Baby Brother) that actually looks like a real little boy.

## Small cars and trucks

Buy safe ones that have plates attached underneath so you can't see the axles, which are small and could be dangerous if removed and swallowed. Little Matchbox and Corgi cars are well designed, inexpensive, and long-lasting.

## Single-shape puzzles

Each piece is one thing to look at. Each piece has a little handle.

# Toys for a two-and-a-half-year-old

### A set of big wooden blocks

A good set of hardwood blocks will last for years and offset in hours of pleasure the initial cost. Supertots like to make towers, castles, towns, roads, tunnels, houses, forts and farms out of the blocks. And there's nothing like wood; plastic, foam, and cardboard blocks just aren't the same.

### Tea set

Buy a safe aluminium or plastic tea set and keep it on a special shelf in the kitchen or dining room so that your child can cook, serve, and do the washing up with you.

### Punching toy

A big, soft, inflatable, heavy-duty plastic Puncho is a good toy for channelling aggression and anger. You can teach your child: *You mustn't hit me, but you can hit Puncho all you want.*

## A set of different hats

Supertots love different hats: a fireman's hat, a policewoman's hat, a cowgirl's hat, a train driver's hat, a dressy hat. Keep them all together in a special box that you open for parades and parties.

## Easy wooden jigsaws

These puzzles should be easy enough for your child to do alone after you have helped a few times. There should be no more than eight easy pieces at this stage. Store the puzzles in a special place when they are not being used; teach your child to put each finished puzzle away before taking out a new one, so pieces won't get lost.

## Train

A small non-electric toy train that can be hitched up and moved around easily is an excellent toy for a supertot. But check to see if your child can hitch it up and unhitch it without your help, and that it doesn't become unhitched when your child moves it around.

# Toys for three-year-olds

### Construction trucks

Good, sturdy
construction trucks
that work with real
sand and soil give
children hours of
pleasure.

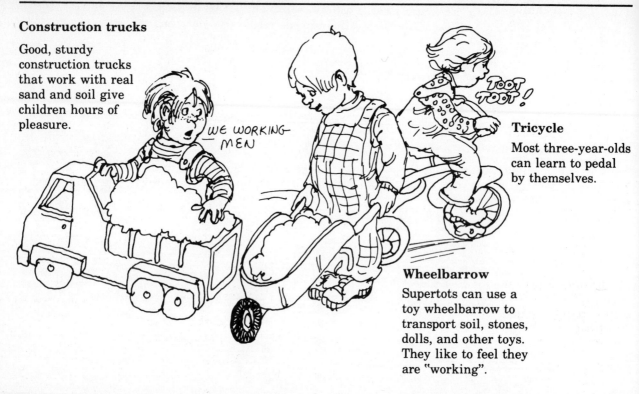

WE WORKING-
MEN

TOOT
TOOT!

### Tricycle

Most three-year-olds
can learn to pedal
by themselves.

### Wheelbarrow

Supertots can use a
toy wheelbarrow to
transport soil, stones,
dolls, and other toys.
They like to feel they
are "working".

YOU WANT SOME JUICE?

## Tools

You can buy toy tools in a fancy tool kit or with a toy tool bench, but you don't need to. The tools are usually a thrill in themselves, and supertots use them to "fix things" around the house. Often the toy bench is ignored.

## Simple lotto games

Lotto, an inexpensive card game in which you match pictures, has many variations; check to be sure the ones you are buying will be easy enough for your child to enjoy.

## Finger puppets

Little puppets that fit on fingers encourage dramatic play, an activity three-year-olds enjoy. The Fisher-Price Play Family figures can be used as finger puppets.

# Good buys

There's a lot of junk about—toys that fall apart and have unsafe pieces that children can accidentally swallow. Since you'll probably often buy cheap toys, develop an eye for good buys such as:

- Safe little cars
- Bubble-blowing liquid
- Small, adult-looking dolls (Tarzan, Batman, etc.)
- Magic Slate (the thing you write on and erase by lifting up the plastic page)
- Fat crayons
- Balls of all sizes
- Blunt-pointed scissors
- Paint-with-water books
- Play-Doh
- Bucket and spade
- Big plastic trucks and cars (some are better than others; find the safe, simple ones)
- Small plastic figures (they come in plastic bags; you can get cowboys and Indians, firemen, soldiers, etc.)

*The toys you buy should:*

- be too large to be swallowed
- have no detachable parts that can be swallowed
- have no little parts that can break off and be accidentally swallowed
- have no sharp edges or points
- be well made
- not be made of glass or brittle plastic
- be nontoxic
- have no parts that can pinch fingers or catch hair
- have no long cords that could accidentally strangle a young child

A brief list of good toy suppliers is given in the Appendix.

MAGIC SLATE

Play-Do

81

# Toy storage

Instead of throwing all your child's toys into a huge toy box at the end of a hectic day, it makes sense, if you can stand it, to sort them out and store them away for future, organized use. Keep similar toys together: little cars in a shoe box or one of those square washing-up bowls or plastic tubs, dolls and doll clothes in another box, snap-lock beads in one container and threading beads in another, and so on. Bring out only a few toys at a time, and when interest in these toys diminishes put them away before you bring out others. The purpose of all this is not to be compulsive, just to make the toys more enjoyable. A toy box filled with all sorts of toys mixed together is not much fun because it's too confusing. The contents beg to be thrown all over the room in order to be seen.

# Ideas for toy storage

### Shelves in a cupboard

On the top shelves, store toys that are used only occasionally.

### Bureau or desk

In the morning you can pull out an entire drawer and set it on the floor so that your child can take whatever he or she wants.

### Cardboard drawers

The nice thing about cardboard file drawers is that they are lightweight and can be easily taken with you on holiday. Plastic tubs are good too.

# Chapter 6
## Art Activities

It's not easy to hit upon successful art activities for supertots: one- and two-year-olds simply are not co-ordinated enough to perform intricate operations with their hands. They can't draw realistic pictures, they can't cut out shapes from paper patterns, and they can't follow directions very well. What they can do is explore materials with great dedication. They'll glue for the sake of gluing, cut paper for the sake of cutting, and paint for the sake of painting. That's quite nice, when you think about it; having no pretensions whatever about making "art", they enjoy the process more than the product.

When you begin an art project, don't make the mistake of thinking it will take the whole afternoon. Thirty minutes of clay or glue or paint is fine for supertots; they they're off to something else. If you keep the art materials handy and easy to use, art activities can be a regular part of your child's life without becoming a big deal.

# First get comfortable

Art activities proceed best and most productively if your child is seated comfortably. Use his or her high chair and tray for this purpose, or buy or make a child-size desk and chair. The nice thing about a high chair and tray is that your supertot can't get out. Not that you want to force him or her to colour or paint; of course you don't, but you do want to calm your child down and help him or her concentrate. Many fidgety twos need to be restrained in order to stop running around; they seem to operate under the principle: where there is a way, there is a will. Naturally, if you child really wants to run around, you should allow this and postpone the art activity for a quieter time.

Uncomfortable: chair too high and table too low.

Uncomfortable: chair too low and table too high.

Comfortable: table and chair just right.

# Stickers

Sometimes they come in the post (Christmas stamps or seals, wildlife stickers, etc.), or you can buy them in stationery shops. Supertots like to stick them on paper. Once they get used to identifying and licking the sticky side and putting that side down on the paper, they can make surprisingly nice collages to hang on the refrigerator. Make sure your child is old enough not to eat the stickers. Ready-gummed coloured paper shapes are good too.

FOR THIS I WENT TO OXFORD?

# Some common and uncommon art supplies

## Crayons

Big, fat crayons are the easiest for supertots to hold. Children can start using them when they're about fifteen or sixteen months old. Keep crayons and paper handy in the kitchen so your child can draw while you cook and wash up. Scribbling is about all supertots do with crayons; don't expect more. They also have a great fascination for putting crayons in and out of boxes, dropping them on the floor, trying to peel off the paper wrappings, and seeing what crayons taste like. Be sure you have non-toxic crayons and that you teach your child not to eat them. (This is easy to teach; simply remove the crayon each time your child puts it in his or her mouth and say: *Crayons are for colouring, not for eating*.)

## Pencils and small pads

Keep a pencil and pad in your handbag for times when you need something to amuse your child. Draw little stick figures and faces, and say they are Mummy and Daddy. Your child will probably scribble on the pad too and call his or her scribbles Mummy and Daddy also.

## Felt-tip markers

Felt-tip markers, both fat- and thin-pointed ones, are pleasurable to young children because they produce smooth, bright lines with little pressure. Be sure to buy non-toxic, *washable* markers; the indelible ones leave *very* permanent stains on clothing.

## Roll-on deodorant jars

Prise off the ball top of an empty roll-on deodorant jar and wash the bottle out. Fill it with poster paint and push the ball back on. The result? A giant ball-point pen that paints.

**CRAYONS** IN THE KITCHEN:

FOR WHEN YOU'RE COOKING BEEF BOURGUIGNON AND COMPANY'S COMING AND YOUR CHILD DOESN'T HAVE ANYTHING TO DO....

**PENCILS AND PADS** *in your pocketbook:*

FOR WHEN YOU ARE AT THE HEALTH CLINIC OR THE DOCTOR'S, AND THERE'S NOTHING TO DO...

**Felt-Tip MARKERS** for special times.

LIKE WHEN YOU WANT TO HAVE A HEART-TO-HEART PHONE CALL WITH AN OLD FRIEND AND YOU WANT YOUR CHILD TO BE QUIET THE WHOLE TIME.....

RED LUE yellow

**ROLL-ON** DEODORANT JARS

WHEN YOU FEEL LIKE DOING SOME-THING DIFFE-RENT, FILL ROLL-ON DEODORANT JARS WITH POSTER PAINT...

# Real clay

Real clay feels good, smells good, and is somehow more satisfying to work than the commercial product known as Play-Doh. When you buy it, ask for a non-hardening, non-toxic clay that is easy to work with and can be used indefinitely. Usually you can buy it at art shops and educational suppliers.

Store the clay in a tightly covered plastic or metal container together with a pair of blunt-pointed children's scissors, some manicure sticks, and a couple of ice-lolly sticks. Keep the clay in the room where your child is likely to use it.

**Some easy things to make with clay:**

- snakes
- worms
- sausages
- pancakes
- peas
- faces
- balls
- snowmen
- monsters

**Other things to do with clay:**

- cut pieces into smaller pieces with blunt children's scissors
- stick manicure sticks and ice-lolly sticks in it
- slice clay sausages into small pieces with a safe, blunt butterknife

**Caution:**

Even though the clay is non-toxic, be sure your child doesn't eat it.

Supervise closely what your child does with the manicure sticks.

91

# Gluing things together

Some two-year-olds like this activity better than others do; they will sit for long periods happily gluing things together. They get glue on themselves; but they don't mind, and you don't have to either, as long as the glue is washable. Actually, the ones who like this activity best are usually the neatest gluers.

## How to get your child started

1. Put a little white glue (PVA) in a shallow plastic saucer.
2. Give your child a basic "bottom thing" (a newspaper, piece of cardboard or wood) to glue things onto.
3. Provide a variety of other things to glue to the "bottom thing" and to each other. Show your child how to dip each thing into the glue and then onto the "bottom thing".

### Good things to glue:

scraps of fabric
advertising leaflets
ripped-up paper bags
pieces of non-crumbly polystyrene
old Christmas cards
old birthday cards

old string
old wrapping paper or leaflets
plastic and metal 35 mm. film cans
scraps of paper or magazines
empty cotton reels
broken shoelaces

## What to do with the finished "collages"

Save them for a day or two; then unless you really feel attached, throw them out. You won't hurt your child's feelings. Save the best ones for the future in a box in the attic; mark your child's name and age on the ones you save.

THINGS
SALLY
CAN
GLUE

# Painting with poster paint

It can be done, but you have to be brave. Two-year-olds *can* paint with poster paint and real brushes; the question is: Can you as a parent stand the possibility of red paint on the kitchen floor? If you don't mind cleaning it up (it's washable) proceed hopefully. If you do mind, give your child felt-tip markers or crayons instead, and don't feel guilty. Your child will get plenty of painting experiences later on in nursery school and kindergarten. And, as a matter of fact, painting experiences for two-year-olds do seem to come off better in school settings anyway. Perhaps it's because there are low, comfortable, child-size chairs and tables in school, and because teachers are more used to painting procedures than parents.

Before you rush out and buy paints and brushes, consider your child's personality and interest level. Exuberant twos are likely to spill the paint as soon as they start and water play with it instead of painting. These supertots are better off with a paddling pool of water and a free rein. Calmer twos, however, can experience the pleasures of painting and concentrate on the activity for a surprisingly long time.

94

**How to get a two-year-old started painting**

1. Spread newspapers on the floor.
2. Dress the child in old clothes or smock. (Old clothes are more comfortable.)
3. Pour liquid, washable, non-toxic poster paint into a few of the hollows in a baking tray (the sort used for small cakes). Fill the hollows only half full. Use only a few colours. You can buy good paint at an art shop or educational suppliers. If you plan to use a lot of it, buy the powdered form; it's cheaper. Baking trays tend to be messy; if you can get them, non-spill paint pots are better.
4. Give your child a fairly wide brush, at least half-inch, with a short fat handle. Have one brush for each colour.
5. Be ready to give your child new sheets of paper to paint on as soon as he or she is done. Lay the finished paintings to dry on newspaper on another section of the floor.

# Fingerpainting

Fingerpainting is fun but messy, and some two-year-olds don't like to get paint on their hands. Others love it with a vengeance. As with painting with poster paint and real brushes, don't feel you have to provide this experience for your child unless you want to. Better not even suggest it if *you* hate the mess. (Maybe you can get your teenage babysitter to like it.)

## How to get a two-year-old started fingerpainting

1. Spread newspapers on the floor.
2. Dress the child in old clothes or a smock. Roll up his or her sleeves.
3. Lay fingerpainting paper down on the floor, shiny side up. (If you don't have fingerpainting paper, use shiny white shelf paper or oilcloth.)
4. Damp the paper with a sponge. When your child gets older and more experienced, he or she can do this.
5. Put a big spoonful of non-toxic fingerpaint in the middle of the wet paper.
6. Show your child how to smear the paint around with his or her hand. Reassure him or her that it's okay to get a little messy.

7. Show your child how to do other tricks with fingerpaint:

HOW TO DRAW LINES IN IT WITH A FINGER

HOW TO DRAW LINES IN IT WITH A FINGERNAIL

• HOW TO MAKE HANDPRINTS ON ANOTHER SHEET OF PAPER

HOW TO MAKE • HANDPRINTS IN IT

• HOW TO MIX IN OTHER COLOURS.

# Sprinkle art

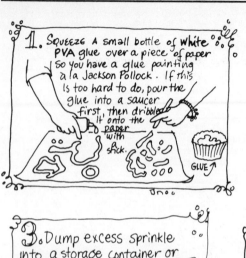

1. Squeeze a small bottle of **white** PVA glue over a piece of paper so you have a glue painting a la Jackson Pollock. If this is too hard to do, pour the glue into a saucer first, then dribble it onto the paper with stick.

GLUE →

2. Sprinkle the wet design with:

glitter
coloured sugar
salt, rice,
confetti, seeds,
pine needles,
or sand.

THE SPRINKLE WILL STICK TO THE GLUE.. SEE?

STICK GLUE...

3. Dump excess sprinkle into a storage container or the **rubbish bin**. If you dump it into a storage container, you can use it for another sprinkle painting.

4. Let the painting dry, then display:

I MADE IT!

**This is easy and produces pleasing results.**

98

# Food-colouring art

1. FOLD A PAPER NAPKIN ANY OLD WAY UNTIL IT IS A SMALL FOLDED OBJECT.

This activity also produces easy, attractive results, but it is a little messy, since the food colouring stains fingers for a while. Eventually the colour wears off.

2. DRIP FOOD COLOURING ALONG THE EDGES, LETTING YOUR CHILD HOLD THE NAPKIN WHILE YOU DRIP, OR VICE-VERSA. USE VARIOUS COLOURS, AND DRIP WHEREVER YOU WANT ON THE NAPKIN.

3. OPEN UP THE NAPKIN. THE COLOURS WILL HAVE SOAKED THROUGH AND MADE A LOVELY DESIGN.

99

## Chapter 7

# Music and Dance

Two good reasons for encouraging your child to sing and dance are: it's fun and your child can do it. Supertots will sing if they are sung to, dance if they are danced with. It's that simple, but *you* have to let loose and do a jig with them every now and then. Don't hold back because you can't do it; a supertot will not judge your abilities to perform. Just have a good time, whether you sing off key or not, whether the dance you do is twenty years old or one you just made up because you never bothered to learn to dance. You may find that one of the unexpected joys of having a child is that you have found someone who will get you moving and singing again.

# Six songs for supertots

You might be surprised to realize that you remember the tunes to all of these. Good! You can sing with your child when you're taking a walk, getting him or her ready for bed, riding in the car, and any other time you feel like it. In case you've forgotten some of the words, here they are. Pretty soon your supertot will know them too.

### I'm a Little Teapot

I'm a little teapot,
Short and stout;
Here is my handle, [Put arm on hip.]
Here is my spout. [Bend other arm up.]
When I'm ready,
Then I shout,
Tip me over [Bend to the side.]
And pour me out.

### Ring a Ring o' Roses

Ring a ring o' roses,
A pocket full of posies,
Atishoo, atishoo,
All fall down!

[Join hands and walk around in a circle, falling down at the end.]

### Row, Row, Row Your Boat

Row, row, row your boat
Gently down the stream;
Merrily, merrily,
Merrily, merrily,
Life is but a dream.

[Imitating rowing motions with your arms, while sitting on the floor, as in a boat.]

## Twinkle, Twinkle, Little Star

Twinkle, twinkle,
Little star,
How I wonder
What you are.
Up above the
World so high,
Like a diamond
In the sky;
Twinkle, twinkle,
Little star,
How I wonder
What you are.

## Jingle Bells

Jingle bells, jingle bells,
Jingle all the way;
Oh, what fun
It is to ride
In a one-horse open sleigh. Hey!
Jingle bells, jingle bells,
Jingle all the way;
Oh, what fun
It is to ride
In a one-horse open sleigh.

[It's fun to shake bells when
you sing this.]

## If You're Happy and You Know It

If you're happy and you know it,
Clap your hands. [Clap, clap.]
If you're happy and you know it,
Clap your hands. [Clap, clap.]
If you're happy and you know it,
Then your face will surely show it,
If you're happy and you know it,
Clap your hands. [Clap, clap.]

[Make up other verses with other
actions: shake your head, touch
your nose, jump up and down,
kick your feet, etc.]

# Real musical instruments

Buying and collecting good rhythm instruments is an investment in pleasure and musical creativity for the whole family. Unlike pianos and violins, rhythm instruments are relatively inexpensive and do not require training to play. They can be played by both young and old; all that is required is a desire to explore sounds and make music.

FIRST BIRTHDAY:
RHYTHM STICKS
SECOND BIRTHDAY:
A SET OF BELLS
THIRD BIRTHDAY:
WOODEN TONE BLOCKS
FOURTH BIRTHDAY:
TAMBOURINE
FIFTH BIRTHDAY:
DRUMS
SIXTH BIRTHDAY:
CYMBALS
SEVENTH BIRTHDAY:
TRIANGLES
EIGHTH BIRTHDAY:
MARACAS

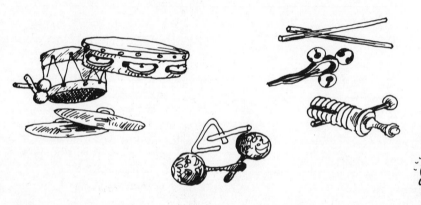

One good rhythm band instrument given to a child each year on a birthday will add up over the years to a fine collection. Buy only rhythm instruments of the highest quality. In most cases, you can't find good instruments in chain stores, but you can find them in music shops or order them from the companies that sell them to schools. (See addresses in Appendix.)

Keep the instruments in a special place, perhaps an old chest or up high on a bookshelf. Don't leave them around like toys. Teach your child to use them with respect; when you finish, put them away carefully so they'll last a long time.

# Improvising musical instruments

When to have a noisy bash with improvised musical instruments: at birthday parties, on rainy days when your child's energy can no longer be contained, to go with dressing up, and when the whole family feels like letting go together.

**Instruments to improvise are all around you:**

1 wooden salad bowl turned upside down
or                                     = 1 drum
1 spaghetti pot turned upside down

1 cardboard paper towel roll
or                          = 1 trumpet
1 cardboard toilet paper roll

TooT TooT

1 ring of metal or plastic measuring spoons = 1 shaker

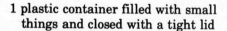

1 plastic container filled with small
things and closed with a tight lid        = 1 rattle

**Hint:** Too much noise may scare small children and give you a headache, so try to maintain a steady, quiet rhythm with your instrument while your child contributes bursts of cacophony. Singing or chanting may give a sense of direction to the noise and may even turn it into music. Marching is another way to provide a sense of musical purpose.

# Dancing together

## Musical Toy Game

Save a musical toy, such as a rattle or
bells, for dancing. Let your child hold it
and make it go by him- or herself. When
the music plays, dance. When it stops,
stop dancing.

## Mirror Dance

Dance and sing
together in front
of a full-length
mirror. It's fun!

ONE
TWO
THREE

ONE
TWO
THREE...

## Exercise Dance

Make up a series of simple exercises that are good for you and simple enough for your child to more or less do with you. The simpler the chant that goes with them, the better. A five-minute routine is about all most supertots can handle.

## Happy Sad Mad Dance

Short expressive "dances" help your child identify emotions and learn how to express and share them. A fifteen-second mad dance can let off steam and find itself turning into a laughing dance.

# Chapter 8

# **Reading Books Together**

Probably the best activity you can share with your child is reading books together. The combination of warmth, comfort, security, companionship, nice pictures, and a good story is hard to beat for sheer pleasure and effective learning. Start reading to your child by the time he or she is a year old, and continue on a regular basis throughout his or her childhood. The Supertot's Reading List on the following pages will guide you in selecting books that are appropriate for your child's interest level.

Early on, casually show your child how books work: how they have pages that must be turned carefully, how the pages start at the front and go to the back, and how the left page is read before the right page. Love and respect for books is a lifelong attitude that children can acquire when they are very young. Supertots enjoy pictures. If the text is too difficult, you can tell the story in your own words.

# SUPER TOTS' READING LIST

*ABC*
Pictures by Brian Wildsmith
(Oxford University Press)

*Alexander and the Terrible,*
*Horrible, No Good, Very Bad Day*
Story by Judith Viorst
Pictures by Ray Cruz
(Angus & Robertson)

*Andy Pandy's Puppy*
Story by Maria Bird
Pictures by Matvyn Wright
(Hodder and Stoughton)

*Animals in Spring, Summer, Autumn, Winter*
Text and Pictures by Vera Croxford
(Transworld/Storychair)

*The Apple*
Story and pictures by Dick Bruna
(Methuen) (*Other Bruna books are good too*)

*A Apple Pie*
Traditional text
Pictures by Kate Greenaway
(Warne)

*Arrow to the Sun*
Story adaptation and pictures by Gerald McDermott
(Kestrel)

*Ask Mr Bear*
Story and pictures by Marjorie Flack
(Macmillan, New York)

*The Baby*
Story and pictures by John Burningham
(Cape)

*Bagpuss in the Sun*
Story by Oliver Postgate
Pictures by Peter Firmin
(Collins)

*Benjamin and Tulip*
Story and pictures by Rosemary Wells
(Kestrel/Puffin)

*Blueberries for Sal*
Story and pictures by Robert McCloskey
(Angus & Robertson)

# SUPERTOTS READING LIST

The Cock, the Mouse and
the Little Red Hen
Story and pictures by Félicité Lefèvre
(Richard Press)

Colours
Words and pictures by Jan Pienkowski
(Heinemann)

Father Fox's Pennyrhymes
Poems by Clyde Watson
Pictures by Wendy Watson
(Macmillan, London)

Goodnight Moon
Story by Margaret Wise Brown
Pictures by Clement Hurd
(World's Work)

Gumdrop, the Story of a
Vintage Car
Story and pictures by Val Biro
(Hodder and Stoughton)

Hugo and His Grandma's
Washing Day
Story by Catherine Storr
Pictures by Nita Sowter
(Dinosaur)

In the Night Kitchen
Story and pictures by
Maurice Sendak
(Bodley Head/Puffin)

Joe and the Nursery School
Story by Alison Prince
Pictures by Joan Hickson
(Methuen)

*The Little Girl and the Tiny Doll*
Story by Aingelda Ardizzone
Pictures by Edward Ardizzone
(Kestrel)

*The Little Red Engine Goes to Market*
Story and Pictures by Diana Ross
(Faber)

*A Lot of Bod*
Stories and pictures by Michael and Joanne Cole
(Methuen)

*Make Way for Ducklings*
Story and pictures by Robert McCloskey
(Viking Press)

*Morris's Disappearing Bag*
Story and pictures by Rosemary Wells
(Kestrel/Puffin)

*A Mother Goose Treasury*
Pictures by Raymond Briggs
(Hamish Hamilton)

*The Mystery of the Missing Red Mitten*
Story and pictures by Steven Kellogg
(Warne)

*Piero Ventura's Book of Cities*
Story and pictures by Piero Ventura
(Random House)

*Richard Scarry's Best Word Book Ever*
Story and pictures by Richard Scarry
(Collins)

*Richard Scarry's Cars and Trucks and Things That Go*
Story and pictures by Richard Scarry
(Collins)

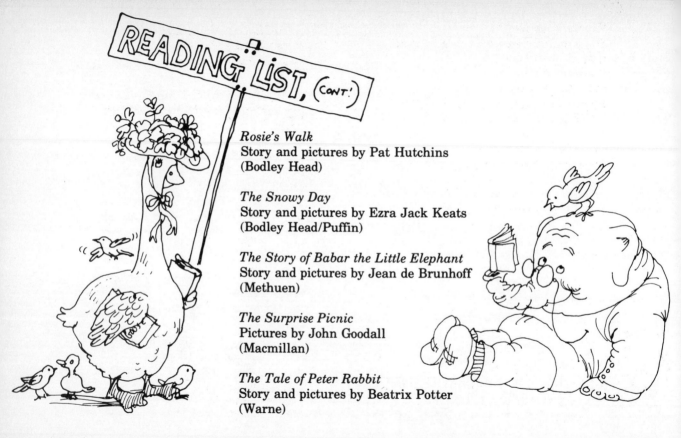

**READING LIST, (CONT.)**

*Rosie's Walk*
Story and pictures by Pat Hutchins
(Bodley Head)

*The Snowy Day*
Story and pictures by Ezra Jack Keats
(Bodley Head/Puffin)

*The Story of Babar the Little Elephant*
Story and pictures by Jean de Brunhoff
(Methuen)

*The Surprise Picnic*
Pictures by John Goodall
(Macmillan)

*The Tale of Peter Rabbit*
Story and pictures by Beatrix Potter
(Warne)

*Teddy Bears 1 to 10*
Story and pictures by Susanna Gretz
(Benn)

*Ten Naughty Boys*
Rhyme and pictures by Hilary Wills
(Methuen)

*Three Jovial Huntsmen*
Story and pictures by Susan Jeffers
(Hamish Hamilton/Puffin)

*Tim's Rainy Day*
Story by Eileen Ryder
Pictures by Angelica Serrano-Panell
(Burke)

*The Very Hungry Caterpillar*
Story and pictures by Eric Carle
(Hamish Hamilton/Puffin)

*Where the Wild Things Are*
Story and pictures by Maurice Sendak
(Bodley Head)

*Whose Mouse Are You?*
Story by Robert Kraus
Pictures by Jose Aruego
(Macmillan, New York)

*The Youngest Story Book*
Selection by Eileen Colwell
Pictures by Margery Gill
(Bodley Head)

# Making your own books

Some of your child's favourite books will undoubtedly be ones you have made together.

### Scrapbook

Cut out pictures of familiar things and paste them together into a scrapbook. Postcards, greeting cards, and pictures cut out of magazines make fine scrapbook additions.

### Photo album

An album of your child's baby photos will help your child watch him- or herself grow up. Supertots like to see pictures of themselves when they were babies.

### Car notebook

Keep some pencils and a spiral notebook in the car for times when you get stuck in a traffic jam and have to wait. Let your child scribble on a few pages, and make a few notes about where you were when he or she made the scribbles and how old he or she was. After a few years you'll have an illustrated history of traffic jams you shared.

# First books

A one-year-old enjoys reading the following kinds child-proof books all by him- or herself:

**Cardboard books**

**Plastic, foam-filled, "soft" books**

**Cloth books**

# Signs

Children can learn to recognize certain words seen over and over again on familiar signs. The idea is not so much to teach them reading at an early age as to get across the notion that words are made of letters and that printed words have spoken sounds and meanings that go with them.

## "Reading" books alone

Certain large picture books (the Richard Scarry books are a good example) are filled with little pictures of things drawn in clear detail on each page. You may tire of looking at these books, but your child will probably enjoy looking at the little pictures over and over again. After you have read the book together a number of times, suggest that your child "read" it by him- or herself. Perhaps you can set aside special "reading-alone-together-times", when each of you reads your own reading material.

## Toy and gimmick books

Toy and gimmick books are appealing to adults and older children, but for one- and two-year-olds they are a waste of money. The reason is that to enjoy them a child must have deft manipulative skills to make them work. Very few twos can pull and push the tabs back and forth to make the pictures pop up. They also find it hard to restrain themselves from ripping and breaking the fascinating paper parts. Puppet books are also frustrating; the fact that the puppets are made of paper gives them a short life with supertots.

# Chapter 9
# **Hassles**

Supertots like the familiar, and they can go along for several routine days being super to live with. But sometimes, if things change, one- and two-year-olds lose their stride; and when they do, they let everyone know it. Anything can set them off: company, illness, rain, frustration with having to share their toys too much, sensing that something is troubling you—who knows? If you are feeling generally okay, you can usually help your child feel better. But if you feel rotten, it's hard. Don't waste time mourning the fact that you are not a superparent in a superfamily. There's no such thing, so don't let the title of this book mislead you. I only hope some of the ideas in these pages will help you cope on awful days and other unusual days, too. Birthday days and new-baby days have their trying moments too. Dealing with the uncomfortable as it comes up can leave you with energy to focus on the expected and unexpected delights of parenthood as they occur. Fortunately, there are many.

# Very bad days when you can't get out

Very bad days happen to everyone. You may be sick, your child may be sick, the car may be at the garage, it may be raining for the tenth day in a row, you may be worried about money, you may be rowing with a spouse or friend, both you and your supertot may be in a rotten mood. The worst thing you can do is take out your rage and frustrations on your child, even though momentarily your child may seem to be the cause of all your problems. The best thing you can do is find a way to get comfort:

- get a baby sitter, if you know of one that can come at short notice.
- forget about accomplishing anything for the day. Cuddle up on the sofa with your child and watch anything on TV together, as long as it's not scary for your child.
- take a walk with your child, even if it's raining.
- call a friend and be honest. Ask your friend to come over and help you get through the day.

# What to feed your child when you can't face cooking

Supertots can be finicky eaters. Don't knock yourself out making elaborate casseroles that they won't eat. Prepare simple foods that are easy to cook: little hamburgers, diced chicken, macaroni mixed with butter and parmesan cheese, spaghetti and tomato sauce, tinned creamed corn, corn on the cob, sliced tomatoes, carrot sticks, whole wheat toast, boiled rice, puddings, and jellies or blancmanges. On a bad day, if you don't feel like cooking anything at all, offer your supertot a limited menu.

NO-COOK MENU FOR A NO-GOOD DAY

COLD CEREAL
OR
PEANUT BUTTER AND JAM SANDWICH
OR
CHEESE AND TOMATO SLICES

BANANAS
APPLES
ORANGES
GRAPES
RAISINS

\*FOR VERY SMALL CHILDREN, CUT EVERYTHING UP INTO SMALL, SAFE PIECES.

# How to keep your child happy when your friends come over

Keep a few favourite toys put away for times when friends call in and you want to give them your undivided attention. Don't make a big deal about it; but after they've said hello, played with your child a bit, and settled down for a cup of coffee, bring out a favourite toy and set it on the floor nearby. With luck, your child will play contentedly alone for a while. But don't expect miracles. If you can get this technique to work half the time, you're doing well. You may prefer to invite friends (especially those who don't have kids) round while your child is sleeping.

# Activities that supertots can do pretty well by themselves

Play with little things (cars, people, animals) and things to put them in (boxes, houses, barns).
Poke pegs into peg boards. (Caution: make sure they don't eat the pegs or poke them into their eyes.)
Play with cars and trucks.
Play with water. (Stay nearby.)

# Getting out and having fun

Supertots are super to live with, but they can get on your nerves.
They are still babies and need you to take care of most of their
needs. They are learning about their own powers, and the main
way they learn this is by testing you. Supertots can, at times, be
dreadful, uncivilized beasts around the house.

Give yourself a break. You work hard at your job of being a parent
and deserve to get out by yourself sometimes. Find a babysitter
you trust, train this person well, and then say good-bye to your
child, push needless guilty feelings aside, relax, have fun, and
indulge yourself.

# NOTES for the BABYSITTERS

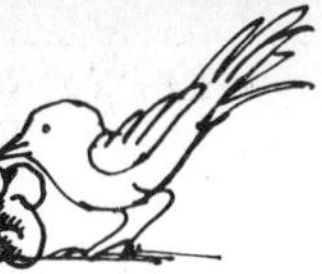

**(Make photocopies of this page and use as needed)**

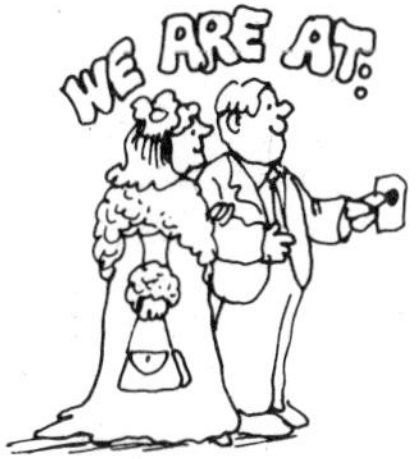

WE ARE AT:


______________________

Address: ______________________

Phone: ______________________

We'll be back at: ______________

**Emergency Numbers**

Doctor: ______________________

Police, Fire, Ambulance: ________

Nearest Neighbour: ____________

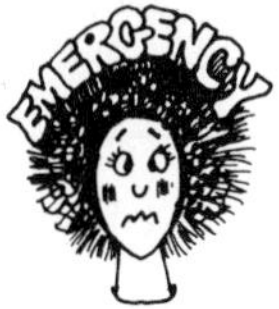

EMERGENCY!


______________________

______________________

Phone: ______________

If you have to summon help, such as fire brigade or ambulance, the address of the house is: ______________________

______________________

Phone: ______________

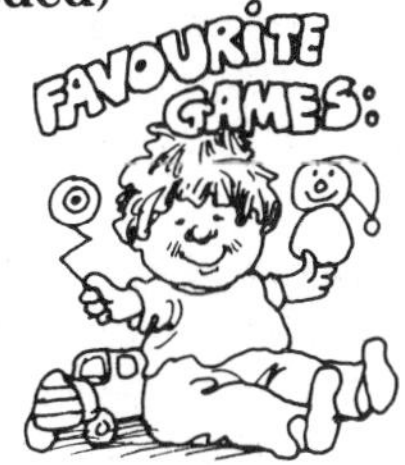

FAVOURITE GAMES:


______________________

______________________

______________________

______________________

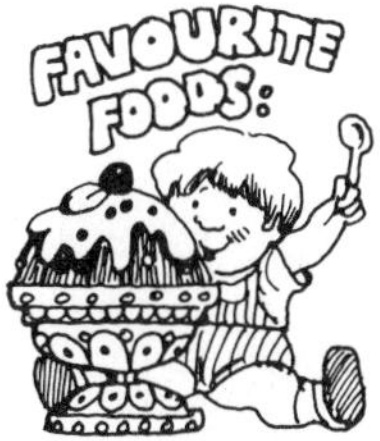

FAVOURITE FOODS:


______________________

______________________

______________________

______________________

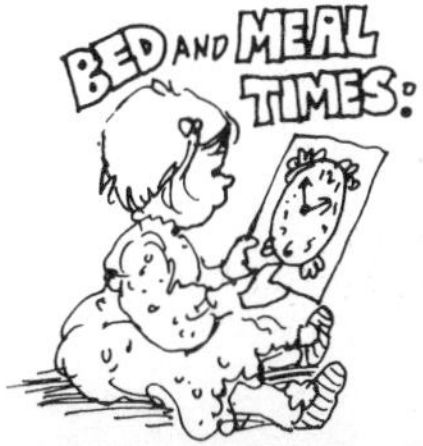

BED AND MEAL TIMES:


______________________

______________________

______________________

# Rainy day idea 1: masking tape

It's raining and the plumber comes and your child is in the way: what can you get to occupy your child while you try to get an estimate from the plumber? Masking tape. Keep a roll of it in the kitchen for times when you can't think. All you have to do is tear off short pieces one at a time and hand them absent-mindedly to your child, who will stick them to his or her tray, hands, clothes, and head quite contentedly.

# Rainy day idea 2: paint with water

This activity, deliberately placed in this chapter instead of in the art activities chapter, consists of painting water on to colouring-book-like pages that already have dry paint printed on them. You can buy magic painting books at some shops and stores; they're good value for money. But know what you're getting; a book that teaches some manipulative skills, but not creative ones. Despite good arguments against providing such non-creative painting experience, it's quite true that most two-year-olds enjoy this kind of water play/paint play immensely. If you save it for times when *you* need your supertot to be quiet, you'll appreciate these books. To help your child avoid spilling, use a non-spill pot and fill it only half full.

# Rainy day idea 3: cards

Brought out infrequently, a deck of cards can surprise and amuse a one- or two-year-old. The reason for bringing the cards out infrequently is: (a) to keep the novelty fresh, (b) to protect the cards from the kind of wear and tear that things get when they're scattered around the house, and (c) to keep the cards together. A one-year-old will probably be interested in seeing what the cards taste like, but a slightly older supertot may enjoy:

Dropping the cards into a cardboard box.

Laying them down on the floor and picking them up again.

"Posting" the cards in a homemade "postbox".

Recognizing some of the numbers. (Children learn the names of numerals and like to pretend to identify them even when they are wrong. You can correct them in fun, but don't make a big deal about teaching numbers at this age. They'll learn them when their minds have developed enough to understand what numbers mean.)

# Rainy day idea 4: a big magnet

A magnet and some metal washers (nails could be dangerous) can be a source of interest on a rainy day. Because the washers are small and because exploring a magnet's properties requires a co-ordinated adult to move things about, this is a good activity to save for when you feel like doing something together.

**Experiments to try:**

Pick up the washers with a magnet.

Put the washers in a box and the magnet *under* the box. What happens when you move the magnet? Let your child try.

Stick the magnets on the refrigerator.

# New baby

It's not easy for a supertot to get used to the idea that a new baby may now live in his or her family. Here are some ideas and activities that can help if your supertot has to make the transition from being an only child to being an older sister or brother.

**Buy or make a baby doll for your supertot**

Put a blanket in the bottom of a cardboard box to make a doll's crib, and suggest that your supertot give his or her doll a name. Buy a baby bottle (a real one or a toy one) so your supertot can feed his or her baby with you.

**Be sure your supertot has a chance to be alone with each parent each day**

It doesn't matter much what you do; just do something together without the baby. Some ideas: go shopping together while a baby-sitter watches the baby, read together, enjoy a suitable radio or television programme together and talk about it, fold the laundry together while the baby sleeps.

## Keep some new toys ready for when visitors bring the baby a present

It's natural for your supertot to feel left out when the baby gets both attention and presents. Your local shops probably have lots of inexpensive things your child would like to get as "older-brother-or-sister" presents. You can bring one out each time visitors come.

## Discuss your feelings about the baby

Talk casually about your own positive and negative feelings about the baby so that your child learns to accept his or her own changing emotions. Be firm about not letting your child hurt the baby. Stop him or her immediately and say, *Hitting hurts. It's all right to get cross with the baby, but you mustn't hit him.*

YOU KNOW... SOMETIMES LITTLE ANNIE MAKES ME SO HAPPY AND SOMETIMES SHE MAKES ME FEEL MAD.

MAD...

# Birthday party for a one turning two

Keep it simple. Invite no more than five children; specify the time the party starts and ends (one hour is perfect); serve juice and birthday cake soon after the guests arrive and before the children get too wound up. You can serve it on a paper tablecloth spread on the floor or lawn. Don't forget to serve something (such as coffee, tea, wine, birthday cake) to the parents too. Take some photographs. If you can get this much accomplished without either you or your child throwing a tantrum, you've accomplished a great deal. Decorations and other extra stuff aren't necessary for your child's enjoyment, so don't bother with them. You don't need special activities either; the other children will be happy to play with your child's toys. Beforehand, explain to your child that several children will be coming to the party and that they would like to share your child's toys. If there are certain toys your child does not want to share, decide together ahead of time what they are and put them away. If you think having a successful birthday party with other children for a two-year-old sounds too difficult, you are probably right. Skip it and have a simple family celebration at dinner-time.

## Ideas for take-home presents

- bells safely sewn on elastic wrist holders
- small, cheap plastic animals or figures
- toy trumpets

# Birthday party for a two turning three

Again, keep it simple. No more than five children, unless some are older and able to help the younger ones play well. Decorations can be fun, especially if your child helps you make them or shop for them, but they're not fun if all they do is create an atmosphere of such excited anticipation that the birthday party itself is a let-down. If you want to initiate a special activity for the party (you don't really need to; the guests will be glad simply to play with your child's toys or with their presents), you can try a parade. Toward the end of the party, give each child a party hat and a noisemaker. See if the kids will march around the room with you.

**Ideas for take-home presents**

· little plastic wristwatches
· little cars
· noisemakers
· party hats

**Caution:** Some noisemakers can be taken apart easily by supertots. The parts inside could be accidentally swallowed so supervise the use of noisemakers carefully.

Chapter 10

# Starting a Mother and Toddler Club

When my first son was one, he belonged to a "mother and toddler club" organized by parents who met each other during the summer in a park. When autumn came and the weather grew too cold for outdoor play, we decided to rent a room and continue our club indoors. The hours were from 9.30 to 11.30, and each of the thirteen children was accompanied by a parent who stayed throughout the session. The children felt secure and liked it; so did the parents. There were interesting toys, safe equipment, warm adults and a casual yet organized spirit. It was out of this experience that I saw how much parents and children can benefit from such groups. There is no perfect way to run one, but in the following pages some suggestions are given that may start you off in the right direction.

# Starting a club in your own home

If you and some friends are interested in starting a supertots' club for under-threes in your homes, you will probably want to meet to talk about various ideas. Start out with the assumption that all parents are different, and stick to practical considerations, since philosophical discussions about child-rearing are apt to end up in pitched battles. A snack can be available for both children and parents, and parents who can sing and know some finger-plays will be popular.

**Goals:** discuss your goals briefly. Two recommended goals are: that the children enjoy themselves and that the children are always safe from physical harm.

**Safety:** discuss safety. Each home should be prepared ahead of time for having a number of supertots playing there. Electrical outlets should be covered; electrical cords should be hidden; detergents and medicines should be put away; stairs and low windows should be protected; tools and other dangerous objects should be out of reach. Outside play areas should be restricted so that dangerous places are out of the children's roaming limits.

**Size:** from three to six children are recommended to start with. Don't start too big.

**Toys:** provide some push and pull toys, some dolls and soft toys with simple clothes, shawls and blankets, a hammer toy, posting-box, bricks and nesting boxes, and some simple books and scrap albums to be shared on a friendly lap.

# Where you can get advice

If you are thinking of starting a mother and toddler club or a playgroup, it is best first of all to contact

**The Pre-School Playgroups Association,**
**Alford House,**
**Aveline Street,**
**London SE11 5DH.**

They will tell you everything you need to know about organizing a mother and toddler club; put you in touch with mothers who have had experience of running a club; and give you the names of other clubs that you can visit and see how they are run.

# Activities that one-and-a-half-year-olds can do together

## Play together separately

Young supertots play separately while enjoying each other's company. Occasionally you have to referee when two of them go after the same toy. Best strategy: distract one of them with another toy.

## Have a snack together

Serve things that don't get too messy: raisins, hard crackers, bananas, apple slices, juice in cups and bottles. (Parents should bring the child's cup or bottle when the child arrives.) After snack, play Pat-a-Cake together.

### Play Ring a Ring o' Roses

This is a good activity for all the children and all the parents to play together. Some children may not want to play; don't force them.

### Play Night-Night together

Give each one a pillow or small blanket to snuggle with.

# Activities that two-year-olds can do together

Everything that one-and-a-half-year-olds can do plus:

**Learn to jump off an old tyre**

**Colour together on a big sheet of paper**

Slide together and walk on a balance board or logs
in the playground, provided they're safe
and not too high

Help you clean up
after snack

# Activities that two-and-a-half-year-olds can do together

Play ball together

Climb on a low climbing structure

Be sure the children are properly supervised, and that the climbing apparatus is safe.

**Learn each other's names and talk about what everyone is wearing**

**Cut or tear paper into scraps and paste down the scraps on a sheet of paper**

This activity works best if the children are seated on comfortable chairs at a comfortable table.

# Chapter 11
# Going Out Together

Going somewhere is usually fun for supertots. They like jackets, boots, raincoats, cars, shops, petrol stations, and visits to other people's houses. They like the variety that new sights and scenes bring to them; they like to talk about what they see. Car trips can provide a different way for you to be together, sometimes talking, sometimes singing, sometimes just being quiet.

Time spent travelling in a car can pass pleasantly for thirty minutes or so before all hell erupts. Your child can't sit any more, is hungry, is thirsty, is wet, is excruciatingly bored. When this happens, stop and provide relief. Most supertots need to take a break from car riding at least once an hour. More suggestions for pleasant car trips and car safety are provided in this chapter.

# Putting on your jacket "all by yourself"

1. Set the jacket on the floor in front of you.

2. Put your hands in the sleeves.

3. Swing your arms up.

4. And let the jacket fall down into place.

# Going to the shops

Ordinary trips to the shop are fun for children and teach them a lot about things you can buy and how people deal with each other. To a child, a shop is a museum, and supertots want to touch everything; so, for your own sake, teach your child that things in the shop are for "looking at, but not touching". Instead of touching, talk together about the different things you see, the people who work in the shop, and the way money is used to buy things. Take your child to different kinds of shops; toy shops, clothing shops, bookshops, shoe shops, bakeries, supermarkets, ironmongers, delicatessens and chemists.

# Car safety

Scrimp on other things, but get your child a safe car seat. Minor accidents which only bruise adults can and do kill children.

**Children are in danger if they are:**

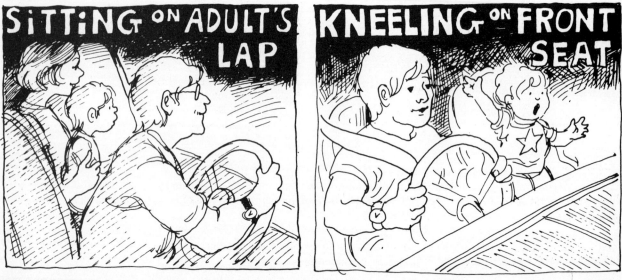

**USING AN INADEQUATE, OLD FASHIONED, UNSAFE CAR SEAT**

**RIDING LOOSE ANYWHERE IN A CAR OR A TRUCK**

**What can happen to them:**

They may be badly injured by hitting the dashboard, roof, or other passengers, even in low-speed accidents or sudden stops.

They may fall out of car doors.

They may cause an accident by bothering or distracting the driver.

# Four kinds of safe car seats

PROTECTIVE SHIELD CAR SEAT

CAR LAP BELT SECURES THE SEAT

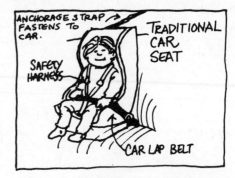

ANCHORAGE STRAP FASTENS TO CAR.

TRADITIONAL CAR SEAT

SAFETY HARNESS

CAR LAP BELT

SAFETY HARNESS

ANCHORAGE STRAP FASTENS TO CAR.

CAR LAP BELT (child must weigh 40 pounds in order to use it safely.)

SHOULDER BELT MUST CROSS CHEST, NOT FACE, OR NECK.

LAP BELT MUST CROSS HIPS, NOT STOMACH.

CHILD CAN SIT ON PILLOW.

# How to buy a safe car seat

The Royal Society for the Prevention of Accidents (RoSPA) has produced a leaflet explaining how to choose the safety harness most suitable for your child's age and weight. Your Local Authority Road Safety Officer will probably have copies of this and may also have some leaflets of his own about road safety.

The address of your local Road Safety Officer can be found at the town hall, in the library or from the Citizens' Advice Bureau.

Manufacturers supply their own information sheets, but before you buy make sure that the product has the kite mark signifying that the safety harness has been approved to BSI 3254 standard.

Install and use the car seat correctly. Otherwise, your money and efforts will have been in vain.

TRAIN YOUR CHILD TO USE THE CAR SEAT AT ALL TIMES. THIS IS PERHAPS THE HARDEST PART. DON'T GIVE IN. BE FIRM ON YOUR CHILD AND YOURSELF IN THIS REGARD. IT'S WORTH IT.

# Supertot's car bag

When you go on trips, keep a supertot's car bag (it could be just a plain old paper bag) in the passenger part of the car. Fill it with:

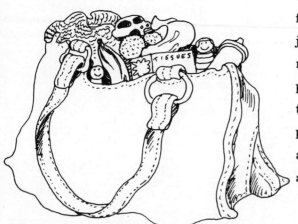

car trip toys and books

food

juice

nappies

plastic bag for dirty nappies

tissues

pre-moistened cleaning tissues

an extra change of clothing

a sweater

This bag plus some good humour on your part plus a child who is healthy should enable you to take a two-hour car trip with your supertot without too much trouble.

But if there is trouble (let's say, for example, that your supertot is screaming his or her head off in the back seat), keep driving calmly until you can pull over to the side of the road. The best thing you can do for your child when he or she freaks out is to keep driving safely until you can stop.

# Car trip toys

Leave some toys in the car so they'll always be there when you need them. On trips lasting more than half an hour, it's a good idea to have someone sit near your child to play with him or her. Not until a supertot is almost three can he or she sit for very long without some sort of diversion. The following toys may provide help.

Ones and twos like to shake and chew on them as they ride in a semi-hypnotic state induced by the lulling sound and vibrations of the car.

To talk with and show things to.

Some children will clutch them for the whole trip.

# Food for trips

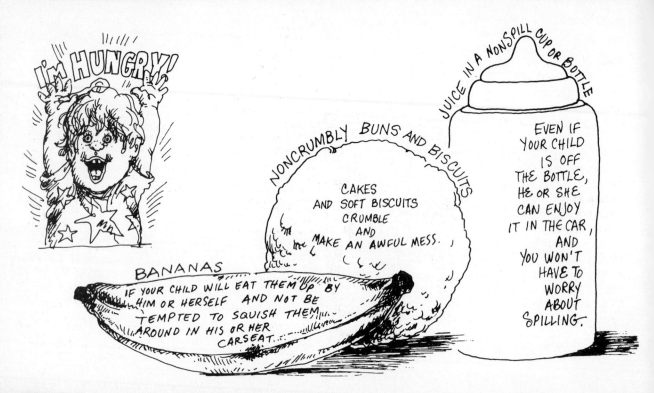

I'M HUNGRY!

NONCRUMBLY BUNS AND BISCUITS

CAKES AND SOFT BISCUITS CRUMBLE AND MAKE AN AWFUL MESS.

JUICE IN A NONSPILL CUP OR BOTTLE

EVEN IF YOUR CHILD IS OFF THE BOTTLE, HE OR SHE CAN ENJOY IT IN THE CAR, AND YOU WON'T HAVE TO WORRY ABOUT SPILLING.

BANANAS IF YOUR CHILD WILL EAT THEM UP BY HIM OR HERSELF AND NOT BE TEMPTED TO SQUISH THEM AROUND IN HIS OR HER CARSEAT.

# Petrol stations

Your child doesn't have to get out of the car to enjoy a petrol station, although stopping at one every once in a while might provide a chance for him or her to get out and take a short walk with you. It's good for children to realize that cars need petrol to go and that cars are machines that have to be taken care of in special ways.

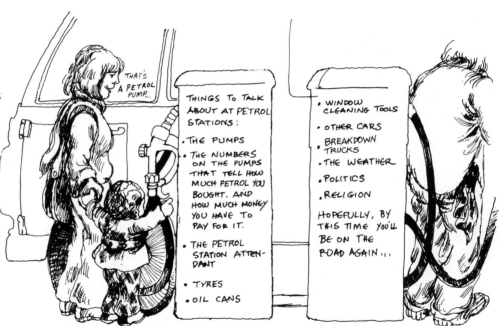

THAT'S A PETROL PUMP...

THINGS TO TALK ABOUT AT PETROL STATIONS:

• THE PUMPS
• THE NUMBERS ON THE PUMPS THAT TELL HOW MUCH PETROL YOU BOUGHT, AND HOW MUCH MONEY YOU HAVE TO PAY FOR IT.
• THE PETROL STATION ATTENDANT
• TYRES
• OIL CANS

• WINDOW CLEANING TOOLS
• OTHER CARS
• BREAKDOWN TRUCKS
• THE WEATHER
• POLITICS
• RELIGION

HOPEFULLY, BY THIS TIME YOU'LL BE ON THE ROAD AGAIN...

159

# Four car games

## 1. Finding cars and trucks

Two-year-olds like to learn the names of different types of vehicles (car, breakdown truck, bus, pickup truck, and so on) and their different colours. After a while, they get pretty adept at describing what they see.

## 2. Shut your eyes

Touching different parts of the body with one's eyes closed is a challenge for a two-year-old and something he or she can practise in the car.

### 3. Chanting the alphabet

Many young children can chant the alphabet before they know what it means. They like to say it as if it were a poem or sing it as a song, and they enjoy the approval such performances produce in most adults.

### 4. Nonsense alphabet

At certain tired, silly moments, making up an alphabet chant from nonsense syllables can greatly amuse two-year-olds.

A sophisticated and more educational version of the above chant is to make the nonsense syllables start with sounds of the alphabet. You can do it only with consonants. F—Foo-foo, G—Goo-goo, H—Hoo-hoo, etc.

# Appendix

## Where to buy toys and things for Supertots

Write to these firms for their catalogues: you can buy direct through the post, or they will direct you to the nearest stockist. Their toys are expensive, but excellent value, and have a play life that spans many ages as the family grows up.

Galt Toys Ltd,
Brookfield Road,
Cheadle,
Cheshire SK8 2PN

Paul & Marjorie Abbatt,
Esavian Works,
Fairview Road,
Stevenage,
Herts SG1 2NX

E. J. Arnold & Sons Ltd,
12 Butterfly Street,
Leeds, LS10 1AX

Community Playthings,
Darvell,
Robertsbridge,
East Sussex TN22 5BR

Fisher-Price Toys Ltd,
P.O. Box 47,
Northampton NN1 2QG

Galt, Abbatt and Arnold all supply paper, paint and other art materials, musical instruments, activity apparatus, and nursery school and playgroup furniture, storage units, etc., in addition to toys.

Mothercare has a good range of medium-priced toys, both small and large; their polythene tractor and trailer is a very popular riding toy.

W. H. Smith and Woolworth are happy hunting grounds for bath toys and small accessories to play in addition to other toys.

**Books for Parents of Supertots**

*Baby and Child Care*, Dr Benjamin Spock (Bodley Head/New English Library)
*Babyhood*, Penelope Leach (Penguin)
*The Child's World*, Phyllis Hostler (Pelican)
*Discovering with Young Children*, Beryl Ash (Elek)
*Feeling and Perception in Young Children*, Len Chaloner (Tavistock)
*The First Three Years of Life*, Burton L. White (W. H. Allen)
*Learning Through Play*, Jean Marzollo and Janice Lloyd (Unwin Paperbacks)
*Living with a Toddler*, Brenda Crowe (Unwin Paperbacks)
*Music with Mum*, Margaret Shephard (Unwin Paperbacks)
*Play is a Feeling*, Brenda Crowe (George Allen & Unwin)
*Running a Mother and Toddler Club*, Joyce Donoghue (George Allen & Unwin)
*The Social Development of Young Children*, Susan Isaacs (Kegan Paul)
*Superkids*, Jean Marzollo (Unwin Paperbacks)
*Understanding the Under-fives*, Donald Baker (Evans)

# Index

*Also published by Unwin Paperbacks*

**SUPERKIDS**
*Creative Learning Activities for Children 5-15*
by Jean Marzollo
Illustrated by Irene Trivas

Designed for kids who like to *do* things, *Superkids* gives specific ideas for projects and basic instructions for carrying them out. Projects like planting a garden, baking bread, making a home movie, planning a party, building a birdhouse. Older children can use this book on their own, younger ones may need help but as they try the various enjoyable activities, they will gain in skills and learn something about their own talents at the same time.

*Also published by Unwin Paperbacks*

**LEARNING THROUGH PLAY**
by Jean Marzollo and Janice Lloyd
Illustrated by Irene Trivas

Play is the natural way children learn and the authors of *Learning Through Play* suggest a wide range of games and activities to amuse small children, that also provide an opportunity to enhance and enlarge upon their skills and achievements. Games for indoors and out, in the car, at the zoo, or on the corner of the kitchen table. Activities that can be easily adapted by playgroups and schools, babysitters, relatives and friends. And most of all, activities that are fun.

Learning Through Play *Jean Marzollo and Janice Lloyd, illustrated by Irene Trivas*    £2.95 ☐
Superkids *Jean Marzollo, illustrated by Irene Trivas*    £2.95 ☐

*These books are available at your local bookshop or newsagent, or can be ordered direct by post. Just tick the titles you want and fill in the form below.*

Name ...........................................................................................

Address ......................................................................................

..........................................................................................................

..........................................................................................................

Write to Unwin Cash Sales, PO Box 11, Falmouth, Cornwall TR10 9EN.

Please enclose remittance to the value of the cover price plus:

UK: 50p for the first book plus 20p for the second book, thereafter 14p for each additional book ordered, to a maximum charge of £1.68.

BFPO and EIRE: 50p for the first book plus 20p for the second book and 14p for the next 7 books and thereafter 8p per book.

OVERSEAS: 85p for the first book plus 23p per copy for each additional book.

Unwin Paperbacks reserve the right to show new retail prices on covers, which may differ from those previously advertised in the text or elsewhere. Postage rates are also subject to revision.